WHAT DOESN'T KILL YA......

ONLY MAKES YOU STRONGER

Navigating Grief: A Guide To Discovering Strength
And Hope On Your Healing Journey

BY: MEKERAH EATON

Publisher's Note: This book is intended as a guide and inspiration for navigating grief and is not a substitute for professional advice or therapy. The author and publisher disclaim any liability in connection with the use of this information.

Library of Congress Cataloging-in-Publication Data

First Edition: March, 2024

Cover Design by Xee_designs1

Printed in the United States of America

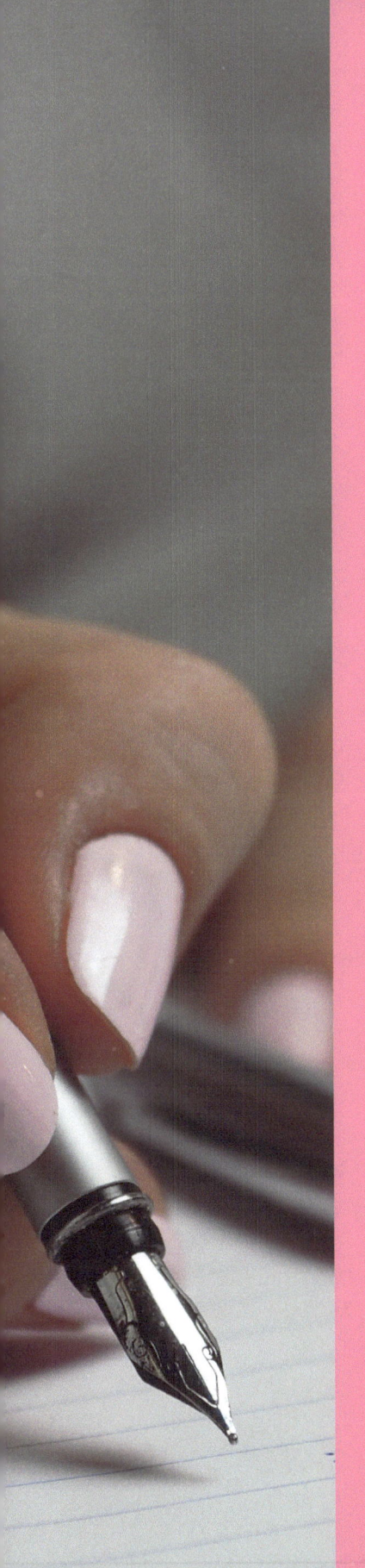

Table of Contents

DEDICATION

In loving Memory

D'jhaii Raymiere Eaton
(December 13, 2013)

I love you Baby Boy and I miss you.
This Book is for you. I wish you could be here to
see what I wrote for you. You truly made my life
better and I miss you with all my heart.

CHAPTER: ONE

What's wrong? What's wrong? Mom, why are you looking like that? Is he breathing? These are the questions I asked right after I gave birth to my son and 2 minutes later he was pronounced dead.

After receiving this life changing news, this is what started my long 4 year journey of grief. After hearing that my son was no longer alive, I didn't feel the pain of loss immediately. I always imagined that losing someone was like how it was in the movies. Where the person would get the call and then fall to the ground with that puzzled look with tears in their eyes. But what I imagined was completely wrong. I say all that to say this book is just to simply help you navigate through your journey of grief in a healthy and progressive way. There is no perfect way to grieve because no one's situation is the same. But I do believe I had a longer grieving process because there wasn't any progression in my journey. I grieved and it took over my life for the worst. I don't want to see others who have experienced a loss go through the same thing. And that's why I believe these 7 practical steps along with trusting in God will help you grieve in a healthy and progressive way. And to whoever is reading this book I'm praying for you in the situation you're facing right now if it's the loss of a loved one, or divorce, or even a job.

I remember that night like it was yesterday. After spending the whole day with my family crying and holding my son, the nurse finally came in and rolled me in a wheelchair to the maternity side and I heard babies crying and people cheering. I remember feeling like a huge failure. I don't really know why failure was my first thought after something that happened that was out of my control, but I believe it was because of my environment. Hearing those babies and people cheering and then realizing I went through labor but my result wasn't the same it made me feel like a failure.

This leads me to my first step:

1. Don't try to Avoid Grief

I felt like a failure in that moment and this feeling of failure I believe is one of the main reasons why I grieved for so long. I went into labor during my finals week in college. After I lost my son I had a choice to take off of school or just go back when things settled down and I felt better. But instead I decided to continue with school because I thought I was a failure and I wasn't about to fail at something else. Now looking back on things I think it would've been wiser to just stay home and be close to my family. Don't get me wrong I don't have any regrets but just knowing what I know now my choice would've been different. I remember having a conversation with my mother and she was basically letting me know what my grandfather said. My grandfather is a wise man and he always gives us words of wisdom. This time his words of wisdom were about me attending school again. He didn't think it was such a great idea for me to return back to school so soon. I disagreed and went back to school full time and was enrolled in 9 classes at the time. I thought to myself if I just focus on school and work I won't have to feel sad and depressed. This was my way of avoiding the process of grief. I told myself that I was fine and there was no point of crying because crying wasn't going to bring my son back. I told my family that I didn't want to grieve. My family thought it was a good idea for me to seek out therapy. I told myself, I don't need no therapy, I'm fine. I don't know if you told yourself this and I'm not saying therapy is for everybody but I know speaking to a professional weekly really helped me get through my grief. Before I started therapy I wasn't getting along with anyone. I was emotionally unstable and it was affecting all my relationships. This was all due to me trying to avoid grief and telling myself lies. So I say to you who are grieving, don't try to avoid grief. It's okay to not be okay. If you feel okay right now, that's great! But grief is unpredictable and it's best to be prepared for it.

This leads me to my 2nd step:

2. Prepare for the hard days in your grief journey

I know this tip sounds unorthodox, and you may be thinking how can I prepare for my hard days in my grief journey? Let me explain. My experience with losing my son was something I'd never imagine would happen. I also found that I didn't know how to deal with a loss because it never happened to me before. I didn't know that some days I would be fine and other days I wouldn't want to get out of bed. I wasn't prepared for the times I would see someone in the store and they would ask me how my son was doing.

Or the times people walked up to me and talked about their children and I busted out crying in their face. To be honest I just thought grief was something you go through and you get over and things go back to normal. Well little did I know and maybe if I read a book like this I would've been more prepared. I didn't take into consideration that grief is something that could be made a little better with preparation. These are the things I wish I did to prepare for my grief journey:

1. Scheduled Therapy Sooner
2. Took the advice of those who wanted the best for me
3. Made a list of things that could cheer me up when feeling down
4. Practiced self-esteem talk
5. Told myself it's okay to cry
6. It's okay to take the day off
7. Don't try to rush the process
8. It's okay to feel what I need to feel
9. Experienced self compassion for myself

My list above represents things I didn't do that I believe that made grieving that much harder. I made the mistake of not preparing for my grief journey and I don't want you to have to go through what I went through. So I ask you at this moment in your life and whatever stage of grief you are in to stop right now and make a list of things that can help you along this grief journey rather it be spending more time with family, traveling more, taking the day off more often, or just scheduling a time to sit down and cry. It's okay if you can't think of anything right now. No worries. But if you think of something eventually, below is a space you can write it down.

Write 3-4 things that could help you on the hard days of your journey.

1

2

3

4

The list you created above are some things you can do to prepare for those really hard days in your grief journey.

CHAPTER: TWO

After I tried to avoid grief and didn't really prepare or become aware of things that could help me in the hard days of my journey, I began to make really bad decisions.

As I mentioned earlier I felt like a failure and I was missing my son. I didn't know how to deal with such great pain. Some days I felt like I just wanted to die. People would ask me how I felt and most days I couldn't even explain the level of hurt and confusion I felt. Sometimes I would just get angry and other times I used sex as an outlet. The anger and sex felt good at the moment, but after the high wore off I was left with even more pain. I self medicated for about 3 years. I was just kind of going through the motions of life until my anger got the best of me one night. I remember getting dressed up that day and hanging out with a friend from school named James. He ran his own business and wanted me to accompany him and show him the big city. At this time I was living in NYC with my bestie. I moved there after I finished school. So I got dressed up and we spent the whole day exploring. So after that we met up with the rest of my friends and we all hung out. The night was great but we had lost the car and my feet were killing me from walking in heels for so long. I began to get angry at different things that took place that night. As soon as I got back to my apartment I grabbed a bottle of wine and began to drink. Each time I thought about something that made me angry I would take a drink. And if you ever got drunk because you were angry, you know those 2 things don't go while together. After drinking a whole bottle of wine, I was so angry about everything but mainly the fact that I was still grieving the loss of my son. I went to the kitchen and began to throw dishes at my apartment wall. I went through about 40 dishes in my cabinet before the police arrived at my apartment. I was so angry about life that I just snapped. I didn't understand at the moment why I was so angry, but later I realized it was because I wasn't getting the proper help for my grief. I had stopped going to church and I had stopped praying and I had stopped believing that God loved me. I was angry with him for taking my son, so instead I tried to help myself. This was literally the worst decision I had ever made. Instead of being angry with God, I actually really needed him to help through the hurt and pain.

This leads me to my third step:

3. Ask God for help in your grief journey

That night I realized that without God helping me through this journey things will get worse. I just think of God helping me as him being a loving father trying to protect his daughter from hurting herself even more. I started to attend church again and pray more. I didn't always feel like praying or going to church but after I would do these things I could see the results immediately.

Sometimes I would go to church and be in so much pain that I would just sit in the back and cry the whole time I was there. But after I left I would feel so much lighter. I would hear God say to me that he loved me. After hearing this so many times from him I began to believe it. I knew that he loved me and that he was going to help me through my journey and he did and he can help you through yours. And what I like about receiving help from God is I don't have to pay money or be a certain person to receive his help.

All I have to do is ask for his help and believe he will help me and it will be done. (Matthew 7:7 for you to read to confirm what I said). Also there is no limit to what God can help you with. What I mean by this is I asked God to help me to get through my grief, but I also asked him to help me with my anger and drinking problem. God started to guide me in all these areas of my life and today I can say I'm healed in all these areas of my life.

Write down 3-4 things you want God to help you with.

1

2

3

4

Now that you have a list of what God can help you with, these are also things you can pray about (prayer is talking to God directly, nothing special, just a conversation asking God for help) especially when you are feeling down about those areas. This step may be new to you but I ask you to try it and look for positive results to happen.

My days began to start to have meaning again. I started to smile more and feel like things would get better. People around me saw the change in me and with that they assumed that my grieving journey was over. The reason why I believe they thought my grieving was over is people would say things like you still feeling bad about that? Or the question would be something similar to that question. After they would ask I would get so offended. I would think to myself how dare you ask me those very insensitive questions. After hearing that question many times I started to believe that I was wrong for still feeling the pain from my son's death. I started to try and act like I was okay even though I knew deep down I still felt the pain so deeply. I even told people that I was over my son passing and I didn't feel anything, just so I wouldn't look weak to them. No matter how much I tried to hide my pain around October every year my behavior would start to change for the worse. I would make horrible and I mean horrible decisions all because I told myself I was okay. This right here is a warning for those who are reading this book.

If you try to mask your pain it will show up in different areas of your life in a negative way. I wanted to be okay so badly and make people feel better about my grief that I lied about my own feelings towards my own grieving process. Now that I'm writing this it sounds so backwards but this leads me to my next step:

4. Please ignore the negative things people say about your grief journey!

It still shocks me till this day that people would even be saying anything negative about something that is so hurtful and painful but it happened to me and I hope and pray it doesn't happen to you. This step is to help those who have already experienced negative comments or people judging you about your loss. So I say please remove yourself from any negativity. I had to learn this the hard way and want to protect you from trying to mask your feelings for the sake of others. In this time you need people who are going to encourage you and uplift you and not worry about when grieving is going to end for you. This is also very important because during my grief process I was super sensitive to everything, meaning a lot of regular everyday situations affected me more than usual. Once I realized this I learned how to remove certain people and things from my environment. This took me a while to realize and therefore it had a huge impact on my grief process.

Below is a space where you can write down things to stay away from during this sensitive time in your life. For example once I realized this step I started to remove drinking from my daily activities. I noticed that when I got drunk It would make me cry all the time and bring out my angry side. I also started to limit my time on watching things that were depressing or scary that affected my anxiety disorder.Everyone is different but I just wanted to give you guys some personal examples so you will have a guide on what to write.

Write down 3-4 things to avoid during your grief process.

1

2

3

4

Quick break:

I just want to stop and say that you are so brave and courageous for even taking these steps forward even in this difficult time. You are awesome and I know God is going to shower down his comfort on you.

CHAPTER: THREE

We as human beings like to be in control of our lives, so when things happen that we can't control we try to still take control in some way.

I like to have control of my life and once my son passed I didn't know how to stop trying to take control even when I knew I couldn't fix things. This was another reason why I decided to go back to college because I wanted to be in control of something. After entering my third year of grief and making some really bad choices because I wasn't getting the proper help, that's when the guilt stage came for me. I tried all the ways to try and control my grief process and stop myself from feeling the pain but once I saw it wasn't working I started feeling super guilty about everything. So let's just put things into perspective. I just lost my son, I was dealing with feeling like a failure, I was also trying to avoid grief, I was also worried about people and how they viewed me in my grief, and I was dealing with anger, and I picked up a drinking habit, and now I was trying to control my life. I was a MESS! And guess what this leads me to my next step:

5. It's okay not to be okay

I know it sounds so cliche, but I'm telling you now that it's literally okay to go through different stages and not be okay. You are going through something you don't understand, and there is no one way to control it and there are no rules. I was so busy trying to do God's job and take control of my life I forgot to ask him for his comfort and guidance. And you want to know another reason why it is okay not to be okay? Because God is on your side. And where you are weak he is strong. AND EVEN WHEN YOU ARE STRONG HE IS WAY STRONGER! I'm going to probably say this more than once because I want you as the reader to understand that feeling the way you need to feel and acting the way you need to act is vital to your grief process. You don't want to skip this part of not being okay like I did. I was acting like one of those people who go to the doctor and then try to tell the doctor how to do their job.

Please learn from my mistake and give yourself permission to feel sad, not get out of bed, eat 50 donuts, cry in your car, cry in public, reserve alone time, watch tv all day, not shower, not do your hair and much more. These things may happen but I'm telling you from griever to another IT'S OKAY. Looking back I wish I gave myself more permission to experience the things that came with my grief journey. Trying to avoid or hide certain aspects about my journey only made things worse. How? you ask, well instead of focusing on getting better and letting grief take its course, I got in the way and tried to control everything. Below are examples of things I wish I gave myself permission to do and feel. I want you to figure out things you're going to allow during this tough time in your life. I'm only putting 5 spaces below but as you're on your journey I know you may have more to add so there is a page in the back of the book for you to add to this list.

Here are 7 things I wish I gave myself permission to do:

1. Spend lots of money on ice cream
2. Not talk to anyone days at a time
3. Not think any thoughts
4. Just sit home and cry
5. Not feel any shame
6. Just be angry
7. Feel no guilt

Here is a space where you can put things you give yourself permission to do during this process.

1

2

3

4

5

The bottom line is that no one has this process all figured out and different days will bring different emotions. I know for me I had to take things one day at a time. This took so much pressure off of me once I began to follow these steps later in my process.

I remember the first couple of days after I got out of the hospital. I didn't know what to expect. Night one out of the Hospital I think I was numb and I didn't want to wake up. I knew if I woke up I was going to have to feel a lot of pain. Fast forward to the week of Christmas I told myself the week before that I was going to be happy. I was thinking this way because I love Christmas and I kind of wanted to put my focus on it. But in reality it was me trying to run and rush the process again. Christmas day came and my whole family took it upon themselves to buy me so many gifts and I was so appreciative but I felt so dead inside.

It was like I wanted to be happy so bad but my mind, body and soul wouldn't allow me. I guess I was trying to force my happiness. Looking back I'm actually proud of myself for at least thinking something positive but what would've been better is me accepting whatever mood I was in. I was so focused on not being a debbie downer around my family because we all love the holidays. But it all goes back to giving yourself permission to feel what you need to feel. I also learned at that moment to not try to predict what mood I was going to be in, just take things one day at a time.

So this is my next step:

6. Take things one day at a time love

Here is a space where you can write 2-3 encouraging sentences that will help you take it one day at a time.

1

2

3

CHAPTER: FOUR

Quick Break:

I just want to say you are strong for making it to step 6. I pray the lord gives you strength to complete 1-6 because loss is unpredictable and confusing but with these 7 steps I want to give you a helping hand to pull you through this tough time. Remember you are loved by God who is guiding you through this tough time.

I used to hate when people used to say this situation is going to help someone else. I didn't care about anybody else at the time. I just wanted to be free from grief myself. It was impossible for me to care about helping someone else because I felt like a load of crap everyday all day. I told myself things like: things will never go back to normal and that I would be depressed forever. At Least it felt like that at that moment. I didn't understand that it was normal for me to feel this way in the beginning of my journey and that I wouldn't feel like this forever. I wasn't familiar with the different stages of grief. I was only focused on how I felt and wasn't really worried about getting better. But this leads me to my last and final step which is:

7. Review the different stages of grief

I'm very hard on myself and since I wasn't familiar with the stages of grief I told myself things like nobody will ever understand what I'm going through. Little did I know that I could search the internet and look at an article that could describe what stage of grief I was in. I told myself all these negative isolation thoughts which lead to my suicidal thoughts. All these negative thoughts kept repeating in my head and they made me feel like giving up completely. I know it was my family's prayers that got me through most days. I was tired of feeling depressed and honestly I was scared out of my mind of my suicidal thoughts, so of course I prayed to God to help me and that's when I started therapy. This therapist was a God send. He helped me with my suicidal thoughts and gave me reading material about the different stages of grief. After reading information on grief and healthy ways to take care of myself my suicidal thoughts went away. I started to get better day by day, month by month, year by year.

It's been 10 years+ since my son passed. I always tell God thank you for getting me through one of the worst times of my life. I'm truly a miracle. I say all that to say THINGS ARE GOING TO GET BETTER! I put that in caps because I want you to know I'm not just saying that but I'm a living witness. I can smile again, I can breathe again, I can enjoy my life again. If you don't get anything else out of this book just remember one thing, God loves you and he is going to take care of you through this journey just like he did it for me, he is going to do it for you. Below is a space to write out the different stages of grief and you can review them to remind yourself that you are not alone! May God truly bless you in this time of grief.

Write out the different stages of grief and review them when you can.

1

2

3

4

5

The next 3 pages are just extra spaces for you to
write extra notes!

ENJOY!

Hello Reader! I hope this book Helps you through this tough time in your life.

If you want to connect to my community for daily support I invite you to reach out to me at strongerwithmeek@yahoo.com for support and connection on your journey. Also, subscribe to my YouTube channel @strongerwithmeek for deeper conversations about hope, navigating grief, and building faith in all areas of your life.

Let's find strength together!

 @prettyprayingwarrior